# Why Are Americans Like That?

# Why Are Americans Like That?

## A Guide to American Sayings and Culture

### 2^nd edition

Stan Nussbaum

Cartoons by Kathleen Webb

*enculturation books*

 Published by Enculturation Books, Morton, Illinois
www.enculturation.org

For permissions, e-mail info@enculturation.org or write to Enculturation Books, 448 E. Delwood St., Morton, IL 61550

Manufactured in the United States of America

ISBN: 978-0-9769146-8-6

Cartoons by Kathleen Webb, www.billykat.com

First printing April 2013

Available P.O.D. book July 2015

Dedicated to

**T.J. and Talia**

the two immigrants I love most

# Contents

# Welcome to America

Welcome to America!
May your American friends be many.
May your studies or your business go well.
May this book help Americans open up to
 you and you to them.

The better you understand American culture,
the better chance you have of adjusting well,
avoiding embarrassment, making friends,
and succeeding in your study or your search
for work. You may not want to adopt some of
the American values you will read about, but
you can cope with Americans better if you
know what their values are.

The 100 common sayings or proverbs in this
book describe many of these values. Of
course, not all Americans share exactly the
same values. Conversations with the Americans around you will increase your understanding of America more than just reading a
book. That is why this book includes many
tools to help you start great conversations.

Look for the large square boxes all through
the book. Everything inside these boxes is for
you to discuss with your American friends.
The questions are all safe to ask. They will
not sound offensive to most Americans,

though they might not be appropriate to ask in your country.

The last box in each chapter ends with some suggestions about movies to watch and discuss with Americans. The movies relate to the cultural values described in that chapter.

The book is written in much simpler English than college textbooks. It also has explanations of the more difficult English words at the bottom of each page, in case you are trying to improve your English.

I hope that in America you will have the privilege of meeting some delightful people like those who helped me prepare the 2nd edition of this book. Anji Sisler, Dan Brannen, Susan Pereira, and Roger Schmidgall gave great suggestions for improving some of the "opinion and experience" questions. Johnny Bruder was a gold mine of information on the movie selections, a new feature of the 2nd edition. Adam Nussbaum ably assisted with graphics and layout. Carole Nussbaum did her usual thorough work as proofreader. My thanks to them all.

We are all glad you have safely arrived in the USA and that you have this book to help you start connecting with the Americans around you. As we say in this country, "Enjoy!"

Chapter One

# An Overview of Ten Key American Values

Here are ten very common sayings that will help you understand ten key American cultural values[1]. I call them the "Ten Commandments of American Culture" even though they are not really "commandments." They have no religious or moral authority like the "Ten Commandments"[2] of the Bible do for Jews and Christians. However, if you break any of these "cultural commandments," many Americans might think you do not fit very well in America. This book will help you avoid the problem by learning to understand American expectations.

While you are learning about American values, some of your American friends may also want to learn about the values of your own country. Please do discuss these things with us. If you can help us understand you better, you enrich our lives.

---

[1] **Cultural values** – what most Americans would consider right, good and normal

[2] **Ten Commandments** – ten rules for life such as, do not make idols, respect your parents, do not kill, and do not commit adultery. They are believed to have been given by God to the prophet Moses on Mt. Sinai over 3000 years ago.

### Commandment 1.   You can't argue with success. (Be a success.)

Success is probably the highest value in American life. It relates to so many other characteristics of American life—individualism, freedom, goal-setting, progress, experimenting, social mobility, making money, pragmatism[3], and optimism[4].

Americans want to "make a success of themselves." This is the "American Dream" which has attracted millions of immigrants[5] and has been taught to generations of American children. Everyone wants to be a success at something. If you do not think that way, you may be considered a failure.

It is almost impossible to criticize success. For example, if an employee does something without properly consulting his supervisor, and as a result the company gets a big contract with a new customer, the employee will get much more praise than blame. The success of getting the new contract will seem far more important than the failure to consult a superior.

Sometimes people will even say cheating is justified if it brings success. Other people, however, may disagree.

*See chapter 2 for more details about success, including a cartoon and some discussion questions.*

---

[3] **Pragmatism** – doing what works to achieve your goal

[4] **Optimism** – expecting good things to happen

[5] **Immigrants** – people who moved to the United States from another country

**Commandment 2. *Live and let live.* (Be tolerant.)**

Americans love freedom and privacy. In a way that means we love to be left alone. We don't want anyone interfering in our affairs, giving us advice, or trying to run our lives. We want people to "stay off our backs," "stay out of our way," and "mind their own business."

Perhaps *Live and let live* should be listed as the first commandment of American culture, even more important than success. It means that no one should object to anyone else's way of living. If you like opera and I like country music, that is fine. If you want to get married and I want to live with someone without marrying her, that is fine too. Neither of us should try to influence the other or object to the way the other lives.

If we are not tolerant of other people, we may damage their self-esteem[6]. To attack someone's self-esteem is to break one of the most basic rules of American life.

> *See the beginning of chapter 3 for more details about tolerance and self-esteem, including some cartoons and discussion questions.*

**Commandment 3. *Time flies when you're having fun.* (Have lots of fun.)**

Americans try to have as much fun as possible. Much of our fun comes through various kinds of entertainment, especially

---

[6] **Self-esteem** – people's view of their own value as human beings

TV and video games. But we also try to turn other activities into fun. Shopping is fun. Eating is fun, and in case it is not enough fun, we will put a playground inside the fast-food restaurant so the kids can have fun playing while the grown-ups have fun sitting and eating.

Learning to read can be turned into fun, as the *Sesame Street* TV programs show. Americans look for careers that are fun (although not many find them). Having fun is the major preoccupation[7] of youth, retired people, and many of those in between.

Usually Americans are very time-conscious. However, we forget to watch the clock when we are having fun. That is why "time flies," that is, time seems to go by very quickly.

*See chapter 3 for more details about fun, including a cartoon and some discussion questions.*

***Commandment 4. Shop till you drop.***

Many Americans (especially American women) shop as a form of recreation. Even if we are not shopping for anything in particular, we simply enjoy looking at all the options. We love the whole process of choosing what to buy and where to buy it. It is a major topic of social conversation. If you want to impress your American friends, ask for their

---

[7] **Preoccupation** – something people think about all the time

advice about where to shop, or better yet, show them that you have already become a "smart shopper"[8].

The saying, *Shop till you drop,* is never used seriously as a command and yet it holds a serious meaning. We are perhaps the ultimate consumer society,[9] and this saying describes us so well that it could be our national motto.

> *See the end of chapter 3 for more details about choices, including a cartoon and some discussion questions.*

### Commandment 5.  Just do it.

We are people of action. We do not like too much planning. That seems indecisive and perhaps a waste of time. We do not like rules and regulations that prevent action. We strongly dislike authority structures where people are expected to inform several other people before they do anything. We get an idea and we want to *just do it.*

Action is seen as the key to success. Action is more valuable than planning, checking regulations, or informing people.

> *See chapter 5 for more details about initiative, including a cartoon and some discussion questions.*

---

[8] **Smart shopper** – someone who knows where an item can be bought most cheaply

[9] **Consumer society** – a society in which buying and selling are the central activities of life and what you own is the main measure of your value

***Commandment 6.    You are only young once. (Do whatever you can while you have the chance.)***

This commandment ties together the themes of several other commandments—freedom, fun, initiative[10] and time. It is a command to enjoy life to the full, taking advantage of every opportunity that comes along. For example, this is why lots of university students flock to the Florida beaches for spring break but the 40-year-olds don't. Adult responsibilities and schedules put an end to the freedom of youth.

*See chapter 6 for more details about youth and age, including a cartoon and some discussion questions.*

 ***Commandment 7.    Enough is enough. (Stand up for your rights.)***

Human rights and dignity are so basic to American thinking that we assume everyone else must think the same way. This proverb implies the command, "Stand up for your rights." In the American Revolution, America as a nation said to Britain, *Enough is enough*, that is, "You have ruled us for long enough. You will not rule us any more."

As we saw in Commandment 2, *Live and let live*, Americans do not want people interfering in their lives. When we sense interference, we push it away.

*See chapter 8 for more details about justice, including a cartoon and some discussion questions.*

---

[10] **Initiative** – doing something because you want to or decide to, not because you are told to or expected to

### Commandment 8. Rules are made to be broken. (Think for yourself.)

We obey rules most of the time, but we see rules as someone else's idea of how we should do things. We think the rule might have been appropriate in some other situation but it might not be appropriate for our situation now. Therefore we break it and do what we think is a better idea. This proverb implies the commandment, "Think for yourself in every situation. Do not just obey rules."

Though Americans say, *Rules are made to be broken*, we never say, "Laws are made to be broken." Laws are official legal "rules" and we proudly claim that in America, "No one is above the law."

*See chapter 8 for more details about rules, including a cartoon and some discussion questions.*

### Commandment 9. Time is money. (Don't waste time.)

We Americans are very time-conscious and very money-conscious. Many of us get paid by the hour for the work we do. We give the employer our time in order to get money.

The idea that *time is money* has gotten into our minds so deeply that it affects our whole lives. Wasting time is as bad as wasting money, so we schedule everything and we hurry everywhere. We often signal the end of a phone conversation or a meeting by saying, "Well, I don't want to take up any more of your time."

If you really want to annoy[11] an American, sit down and talk as if you have nothing else to do for the rest of the day. You will be breaking the ninth commandment of American culture, "Don't waste time."

*See chapter 9 for more details about time, including a cartoon and some discussion questions.*

***Commandment 10. God helps those who help themselves. (Work hard.)***

In a list of "Ten Commandments," one might expect that God would be mentioned in the first commandment rather than the last one. But in American culture, God actually does come at the end of the list. For most Americans, God is much less a concern than success, money and time. (There are many Americans who put God at the top of their personal list of priorities,[12] but they are a minority within American culture.)

*God helps those who help themselves* could mean, "God rewards people who work hard" or it could mean, "God doesn't really help anyone. Your success depends on you, not God." Either way, the proverb points to the same commandment, "Whether you believe in God or not, work as hard as you can." It is better to be independent than to depend on other people.

*See chapter 10 for more details about God, including a cartoon and some discussion questions.*

---

[11] **Annoy** – bother, make someone angry with you

[12] **Priorities** – things that are important, often listed with the most important one first

## *Ask your American friends*

### *Opinions and experiences*

**?**  *If you had to pick one or two say-ings that almost everyone in America lives by, which would you pick from this list and why:*

- *You can't argue with success.*
- *Live and let live.*
- *Time flies when you're having fun.*
- *Shop till you drop.*
- *Just do it.*

### *A movie to watch and discuss*

*Star Wars: A New Hope.* (1977, sci-fi, PG) Though no one movie can give a complete picture of American values, *Star Wars* epitomizes[13] much of the American dream—one ordinary farm boy using courage, ingenuity, technology, and "the Force" to fight and defeat a cosmic evil empire.

The name "*Star Wars*" applies both to the single movie released in 1977 and to the whole series of six movies from 1977-2005. The 1977 movie is also known as *"Star Wars Episode IV: A New Hope."* Three more movies are planned for the series from 2015 onward.

---

[13] **Epitomizes** – summarizes or embodies. "She is the epit-ome of kindness."

## Chapter Two

# The Top Priority in American Life

The "American Dream" is a dream of individual success. That is the top priority for many of us. We know that the dream has come true for many "self-made" people. They have set their goals. Their hard work has paid off. The whole nation admires their achievements especially if they came from ordinary or poor backgrounds like Henry Ford, Marilyn Monroe, Billy Graham, Oprah Winfrey and Michael Jordan all did.

Success stories like these inspire us all to try to make a success of ourselves. We dream big dreams. Children all over America are practicing basketball, imagining themselves as the next Michael Jordan. More than anything else in life, we Americans want our biography[1] to be a success story, and the bigger, the better.

### *Ask your American friends*

#### *Opinions and experiences*

**?**  *Can you name two or three people you would consider very successful Americans? Why do Americans admire these people so much?*

---

[1] **Biography** – the story of someone's life

> **?** *May I tell you which Americans are most admired in my country?*
>
> **?** *What kinds of things do Americans have in mind when they talk about "being a success"?*
>
> **?** *Do you think America is the most successful country in the world? How do you measure "success" for a country?*

## Success as an Ideal

1. [2] *(Commandment 1) You can't argue with success.* Though you may tell someone they are doing something in a wrong way, you have to stop criticizing them if their method works.

2. *Nothing succeeds like success.* Like money in a savings account, success seems to compound[3] itself. A person who has a small success expects it to be followed by a bigger one.

3. *Go for it.* Go ahead and try to achieve your goal. Don't worry about failing.

Americans have been described as pragmatists, that is, people who care more about success than anything else. Another way of saying this is, *"You can't argue with success."* This is what we call the "First Commandment" (most basic principle) of American culture.

Since success is so important, we spend a lot of time and energy setting goals. The goals help us focus our lives and measure our success.

---

[2] The symbol is a reminder of the original Ten Commandments written on stone. It marks the most important sayings.

[3] **Compound** – multiply over and over

"Mission statements"[4] have become popular in American business. Even schools and hospitals write "mission statements."

Very few of us sit down and write out a personal "mission statement" but we do constantly set goals for ourselves. They can be huge life-long goals or tiny goals like getting three errands finished by 10:00. We measure ourselves by these goals. If we fail to reach our goals, we experience stress and frustration.

To understand any particular American, learn what his or her goals are. If you can help an American toward an important goal, you will be treated very well.

---

## *Ask your American friends*

### *Opinions and experiences*

**?**  *Americans seem to have big dreams and to think about goals a lot. What kinds of dreams or goals do you have for yourself this month or this year? Do you have goals for your whole life?*

**?**  *Can you give me an example of a "mission statement"? Why would a hospital have to write a mission statement and post it on the wall? Isn't it obvious what a hospital is supposed to do?*

### *Other proverbs to discuss*
*(share some from your country too)*

~  *The end justifies the means.*

~  *All is well that ends well.*

---

[4] **Mission statements** – one-sentence summaries of an organizational goal

~ *Killing two birds with one stone.*

~ *All's fair in love and war.*

~ *Always a day late and a dollar short.*

## CARRYING OUT A STRATEGY

4. *There's many a slip between the cup and the lip.* This refers to a plan that has gone wrong. When one is drinking from a cup, one intends to get all the drink into the mouth, but this does not always happen. The plan is good but it can still fail.

5. *One thing at a time.* Concentration leads to success. The person who tries to do too many things at once may fail at all of them.

6. *When in Rome, do as the Romans do.* Flexibility leads to success in unfamiliar circumstances. People may change their normal way of doing things in order to fit in better with those they are visiting.

7. *Don't put the cart before the horse.* Do things in a sensible order. For example, do something to impress your boss before you ask for a raise in pay. Don't ask for the raise first.

Once a goal is set, an appropriate strategy[5] may be chosen. This choice has to be made very carefully because a good strategy will bring success and a poor strategy may lead to failure.

A strategy has to combine the right amounts of many different values described in the proverbs. Some of these are concentration, flexibility and common sense. The wise person

---

[5] **Strategy** – a careful plan for achieving a goal

knows how much of each one is needed to bring success in each situation.

Ambition, self-confidence and hard work are required while a strategy is carried out. We will discuss these in later sections. Success such as winning the lottery[6] may be envied but it is not admired because it comes through sheer luck rather than strategy or effort.

---

## *Ask your American friends*

### *Opinions and experiences*

**?** *Suppose I wanted to live by the saying, "When in America, do as the Americans do." What should I learn to do in an American way? What will help me fit in? What will make me stick out like a foreigner?*

### *Other proverbs to discuss*
*(share some from your country too)*

~ *There is more here than meets the eye.*

~ *Easy does it.*

~ *Don't count your chickens before they are hatched.*

---

### TAKING RISKS CAUTIOUSLY

8.  *Look before you leap.* Do not jump into a situation carelessly. You may land in difficulty.

9.  *Too good to be true.* This is often used to warn about advertising. An offer looks good but turns out to be misleading.

---

[6] **Lottery** – a type of gambling run by the governments of some US states. A winner may receive millions of dollars.

**10.** *There is no such thing as a free lunch.* Similar to the previous proverb. If someone you do not know offers you a free lunch or other gift, watch out. The gift may be a method of getting something from you.

**11.** *Time will tell.* Wait and see how something will work out. Do not trust a person or thing too much right now.

**12.** *Don't bite off more than you can chew.* Don't attempt something too large for you to handle.

Being great risk-takers, Americans have a lot of experience with strategies that go wrong. We have many proverbs that warn us about what to keep in mind when we take risks. *Look before you leap (8).* Realize that something that looks good might be *too good to be true (9).*

Risk-taking is usually admired but not if it is foolish. An overconfident[7] person may be warned, *Don't bite off more than you can chew (12).* Don't take an advanced chemistry course if you did not do well in the basic chemistry course.

---

## *Ask your American friends*

### *Opinions and experiences*

**?** *Can you give me an example of a time when you did something risky and it worked out OK?*

**?** *How about a time when you took a risk and then wished you hadn't?*

---

[7] **Overconfident** – thinking you can do great things that you really cannot do

*Other proverbs to discuss*
*(share some from your country too)*

~ *Curiosity killed the cat.*

~ *All that glitters is not gold.*

~ *Seeing is believing.*

~ *Where there's smoke there's fire.*

~ *Better safe than sorry.*

~ *Don't put all your eggs in one basket.*

~ *A bird in the hand is worth two in the bush.*

~ *Pride goes before a fall.*

~ *Hindsight[8] is always 20/20.[9]*

~ *The burned child shuns fire.*

~ *Once bitten, twice shy.*

### BEING CONFIDENT AND DETERMINED TO SUCCEED

13. *Where there's a will, there's a way.* Any problem can be solved if one is determined enough.

14. *So far so good.* Said by or to someone who is carrying out a plan taking one step at a time. Confidence increases with each step.

---

[8] **Hindsight** – looking back on a situation

[9] **20/20** – proper, clear eyesight. The numbers are used by eye doctors to describe how clear or poor a person's vision is.

15. *Yes we can.* The 2008 campaign slogan of Barack Obama summarized American optimism and helped him win the presidency.

16. *When the going gets tough, the tough get going.* When the situation is difficult, the determined people can handle it. They do not give up.

17. *If you can't beat 'em, join 'em.* If you cannot compete successfully with a person or group, stop competing and go join them. Then you can share in their success.

As we push for success, we think that almost anything is possible. We encourage each other to take risks. Perhaps this is because we are mostly people (or descendants[10] of people) who left the land of their forefathers and moved to America because it offered a better future for them and their children. That was a huge risk. For most Americans, that risk paid off. Today we are a nation of risk-takers—look how many of us put our money into the stock market!

Our confidence helps us handle the set-backs[11] that come with risks. We do not lose sight of our goal. We tell ourselves, *When the going gets tough, the tough get going (16).* Perhaps the setback came because we did not make our first attempt in the best way. Perhaps the task was too big or the time was not

---

[10] **Descendants** – children, grandchildren, great-grandchildren and all the later people who can trace their family line back to the same person

[11] **Set-backs** – events that "set you back," that is, things that push you farther away from your goal instead of bringing you closer to it

right. We need to be patient and determined. We have to "hang in there."

Once in a while we do have to admit that we cannot achieve a goal, no matter how we try. We give up on it, but we do not stop setting other goals. To us, that would be giving up on life and starting down the road to suicide,[12] the ultimate failure. Instead, we simply set a different goal and start looking for a strategy to succeed at that. We may even leave one group and join a different group in order to have a better chance of success the next time. *If you can't beat 'em, join 'em (17).*

## *Ask your American friends*

### *Opinions and experiences*

**?** *Americans seem to have a "can do" attitude[13] toward life. You say,* Where there's a will, there's a way. *Can you think of an experience where things did not work for you at first but you kept trying different approaches until you made progress?*

**?** *How closely do you agree with this proverb:* When the going gets tough, the tough get going? *Is that how you live your life?*

### *Other proverbs to discuss*
(share some from your country too)

---

[12] **Suicide** – killing oneself

[13] **"Can do" attitude** – confidence. The attitude that says, "I can do this."

~ *The sky is the limit.*

~ *We'll cross that bridge when we come to it.*

~ *Every little bit helps.*

~ *If at first you don't succeed, try, try again.*

~ *While there is life there is hope.*

~ *It isn't over till the fat lady sings.*

~ *Rome wasn't built in a day.*

~ *There are other fish in the sea.*

## Movies to watch and discuss

*Forrest Gump* (1994 romantic comedy-drama, PG-13). A disabled, disadvantaged, unintelligent boy lives by the advice of his single mother and grows to become a star athlete, war hero, successful businessman, and the father of an intelligent son.

Other options: *Karate Kid, Trading Places, The Pursuit of Happyness[14], On the Waterfront, The Sound of Music*

---

[14] "Happyness" is deliberately misspelled in this movie title. The normal spelling is "happiness."

Chapter Three

# Self-esteem and Fun

Success is probably the top priority for most Americans, but self-esteem[1] and fun are valued almost as much. One cannot understand Americans without realizing this.

## SELF-ESTEEM—THE DIGNITY OF THE INDIVIDUAL

18. *(Commandment 2) Live and let live.* Do not be judgmental. Do not try to control or punish other people. You live as you like and let others live as they like.

19. *Looking out for number one.* Protecting yourself carefully, even if you hurt others in the process. This is sometimes used to criticize a person who has abused or taken advantage of someone else, "All he was doing was looking out for number one." Or it may be used by a person to defend himself or herself, "There is nothing wrong with what I did. I was just looking out for number one."

20. *The customer is always right.* Businesses instruct their clerks not to do anything that might threaten a customer's self-esteem, no matter how unreasonable the customer is. Any complaint of any customer must be carefully and politely heard by any employee. The customer must not be made to feel ignorant.

---

[1] **Self-esteem** – your opinion of yourself

Though there are far more proverbs about success than self-esteem, the few proverbs about self-esteem are crucial to American thinking. The three proverbs quoted above are the foundation for the American understanding of everything that is normal, good and right.

Americans think it is natural and healthy for every person to be *looking out for number one (19)*. From kindergarten[2] onward, schools and parents tell children how "special" each one is. Even if children do poorly in their school work, teachers avoid giving them low or failing grades because that may damage their self-esteem, that is, their sense of self-worth. They will feel like failures, not successes. The philosophy of life is, "Express yourself," "Enjoy yourself," "Respect yourself," and "Be true to yourself."

Like a desire for success, self-esteem can be seen as a core value of American culture. Self-esteem, which is closely related to personal dignity, is often seen as the most basic human right and the key mark of a psychologically healthy person. Nobody wants to have low self-esteem, and nobody wants to associate with people who do.

Whatever promotes self-esteem is good and whatever diminishes it is bad. That is why racism, sexual harassment, child abuse, male chauvinism[3] and religious intolerance are

---

[2] **Kindergarten** – the first year of school, usually at age 5

[3] **Male chauvinism** – the belief that men are more important than women

so unacceptable in America today. They all attempt to assert one person's dignity or power in a way that tears down the dignity of others.

This is also the reason that Americans like to be called by their first name rather than their title, except in special cases such as judges, doctors and the military. We do not want to make others feel inferior[4] to us since that would cause self-esteem problems for them.

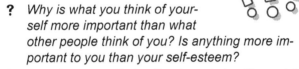

## Ask your American friends
### Opinions and experiences

**?**  *Why is what you think of your-self more important than what other people think of you? Is anything more important to you than your self-esteem?*

**?**  *Americans say that self-esteem is healthy, yet they do not like people who are arrogant or "stuck up." What is the difference between self-esteem and arrogance? What are the best and worst ways to try to build self-esteem?*

**?**  *Is* looking out for number one *always a good thing? Is that how most Americans live?*

### Other proverbs to discuss
*(share some about your own country too)*

~  *To each his own.*

~  *Be true to yourself.*

**See also**: *Celebrate diversity (53).*

---

[4] **Inferior** – of lower quality or less importance

## Fun

**21.** *(Commandment 3) Time flies when you're having fun.* A day seems short when it is full of enjoyable things but it seems like an eternity[5] if one is idle or stuck with a boring job.

**22.** *If it feels good, do it.* Live according to your desires at the moment. Forget about rules, regulations or consequences. Just have fun.

**23.** *Are we having fun yet?* This is a sarcastic[6] question. People who really are having fun do not have to ask such a thing. The question calls attention to the fact that something is not fun at all.

Some people build their whole lives around fun. They say, *If it feels good, do it (22).* Though most Americans do not go quite that far, we do spend a lot of time looking for ways to have more fun.

Weekend time is fun time. Families have fun together. On vacations people go wherever they will have the most fun. Sex is fun. New experiences are fun. Hobbies are fun. The people we like are the ones who are "fun to be with." We even say, "She's a fun person." We wish that our whole lives were fun, and they would be (we think) if we did not have to spend so much time working.

Americans are so individualistic that it seems that golf and tennis would be more fun for us than other sports. For some strange reason we love team sports in which everything depends

---

[5] **Eternity** – an endless period of time

[6] **Sarcastic** – containing a hidden insult

upon each member of the group playing his or her role in constant and perfect harmony with other team members. This is particularly true of American football and basketball.

We seem to recognize that, like success, fun is even more enjoyable when it is shared with other people. That may happen with a sports team, at a party, or just with a good friend, a husband or a wife.

## *Ask your American friends*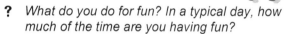

### *Opinions and experiences*

? *What do you do for fun? In a typical day, how much of the time are you having fun?*

? *Who are your favorite friends to have fun with? Where do you go together and what do you do there?*

? *Are you a fan of any professional sports team? Why do you like that sport and that team?*

? *Is it possible to invest too much time and energy in sports entertainment?*

### *Other proverbs to discuss*
*(share some about your own country too)*

~ *You only go around once in life.*

~ *All work and no play makes Jack a dull boy.*

~ *The more the merrier.*

~ *It takes two to tango.*

## CONFLICTS AMONG THE THREE PRIMARY GOALS

**24.** *You can't have your cake and eat it too.* Make up your mind. Sometimes one must choose between two very desirable things, giving up one in order to enjoy the other. If you have a piece of cake, you can save it to eat later. If you eat it now, you do not have it any more.

Individual success, self-esteem and fun may not be achievable at the same time. For example, success in a career may require such long working hours that the person has no time or energy left for fun. The person is a "workaholic."[7] On the other hand, if a student spends too much time having fun, he or she may flunk out[8] of college.

Success may also clash with self-esteem if the success comes through competition. Some educators have applied this to athletic games in grade school and prohibited[9] anyone from keeping score. The point of the game is not success but participation which builds self-esteem.

Self-esteem and fun may also conflict with each other. A bigger waistline means a smaller self-esteem, but dieting is never as much fun as eating.

---

[7] **Workaholic** – a "workaholic" is addicted to work as an "alcoholic" is addicted to alcohol

[8] **Flunk out** – fail so many courses that one is dismissed from school

[9] **Prohibited** – made a rule against

**Ask your American friends**

**Opinions and experiences**

? My book says that success,
 self-esteem and fun are three of the most important things in American life. How true is that for
 you or the people you know?

? Do you know many "workaholics" (people who
 pour all their time and energy into their work)? Do
 you pity them, admire them or have some other attitude toward them?

## JUST THREE GOALS BUT THOUSANDS OF VARIATIONS

Success, self-esteem and fun are common
cultural goals, but each American gets to
choose his or her own definition of these
things. For example, making lots of money
may mean success to one person but not to
another. Swimming may be fun for one person but boring for another. When we consider our choices, we love to have lots of options. This is true in every aspect of life.

25.  (Commandment 4) Shop till you drop.
 Shopping is a form of considering options.
 We think this is fun so we keep doing it
until we are worn out. This saying is often used
playfully, though it may take on more serious
tones at Christmas[10]—the only time of year
when shopping seems to be a chore.

---

[10] **Christmas** – December 25th, when Christians celebrate
the birth of Jesus, the "Christ." Americans commonly give
gifts to friends and family on Christmas Day. American
stores are busiest in December.

**26.** *Variety is the spice of life.* Variety is what makes life pleasurable. Boredom is seen as a threat and monotony[11] is the surest route to boredom.

Though there may be no proverb (yet) which says so, American life seems to go by the principle, "More choices mean a better life." The saying, *Variety is the spice of life (26)*, comes close to it, but spice is merely something nice. Life does not depend on spice. By contrast, choice is the "bread and butter" (the basic necessity) of American life.

Multiplication of options and choices is evident everywhere in America. There are 400 TV channels available on one satellite hook-up, hundreds of pictures and designs one can have imprinted on personal checks, dozens of flavors and types of dog food in the local grocery store, and a bewildering list of kinds of dressing you can have on your salad at the restaurant.

This is why we say, "*Shop till you drop.*" Shopping can be exhausting when there are so many things to choose from. The customer also gets used to the idea, "Some store somewhere has exactly what I am looking for (and maybe at a better price), so I won't buy this item which is almost right. I will keep looking." On we go to the next store.

Our desire for more choices is one of the main reasons more and more of us live in urban and suburban areas rather than small towns or rural areas. One has more choices in a city.

---

[11] **Monotony** – doing the same thing over and over

## *Ask your American friends*

### *Opinions and experiences*

**?** *Why do Americans like it so much when they can get 500,000 apps for their phone instead of 300,000 or 400 channels on their TV instead of 200? What do more choices and options represent to Americans?*

**?** *If you were offered a job with reasonable pay in a town of 1000 people, how seriously would you consider it?*

### *Other proverbs to discuss*
*(share some about your own country too)*

~ *There is more than one way to skin a cat.*

~ *One man's meat is another man's poison.*

### *Movies to watch and discuss*

*Precious* (2009 drama, R). A young black girl, viciously abused by both her parents, regains her self-esteem through a teacher at a special school.

Other options: *The Breakfast Club, The Silver Linings Playbook, How to Train Your Dragon*

Chapter Four

# Ways To Achieve
# Three Goals at Once

Of course we Americans would like to enjoy success, self-esteem and fun all at the same time with no conflict between them. We think we know at least three ways of achieving this—love, money, and playing to win. These are so important that some of us even value them for their own sake rather than as means to the three goals of success, self-esteem and fun.

## LOVE

27. *Love conquers all.* Love overcomes all difficulties. For example, if a wife becomes crippled,[1] the husband's love conquers that problem. He continues to care for her and be faithful to her.

28. *Love finds a way.* Similar to previous proverb. Love is considered one of the most powerful and determined forces in the world. Two people in love will "find a way" to get together.

29. *Love makes the world go 'round.* Love is the driving force in all of life. Love makes life worth living. If you understand love, you understand everything about life.

---

[1] **Crippled** – unable to walk

Love and sex feature very largely in American movies, music, and other aspects of culture. They represent an obvious way to achieve all three primary cultural goals at the same time—success, self-esteem and fun.

Most Americans still see it as a success to have a steady, enjoyable love relationship, (and some men even think it is a "success" whenever a woman goes to bed with them). A person's self-esteem goes up when he or she is loved by someone desirable. And sex is fun, along with all the flirtations leading up to it. At least that is how it is in the movies.

You may get the impression from some Americans that the most important thing in life is to "fall in love," "be in love" and enjoy sex. Yet we Americans have big problems with love because we keep trying to mix it with our individualism. The mix usually does not work out the way we think it should.

That is why we have so many popular songs that say love lasts forever and so many other songs that wail about love that was betrayed,[2] abandoned or lost. We even have one song called, "The Greatest Love of All." It is not about love for a lover. It is about "learning to love yourself"! This is individualism gone wild.

---

[2] **Betrayed** – cheated on by someone you trusted. The person secretly breaks promises to you or helps your enemies.

## *Ask your American friends*

### *Opinions and experiences*

**?** *Do you think that people who are in love have a higher self-esteem than people who are not in love? Should they?*

**?** *Lots of American songs talk about love lasting forever but lots of other songs talk about broken hearts and lost loves. Which view is right? When people fall in love, do they stop looking out for number one or not?*

### *Other proverbs to discuss*
*(share some about your own country too)*

~ *Love is blind.*

~ *Absence makes the heart grow fonder.*

~ *Out of sight, out of mind.*

~ *Marry in haste and repent at leisure.*

### MONEY

**30.** *Money talks.* Wealth has influence. People who make big donations to political candidates are "talking" to the candidates and expecting them to listen.

**31.** *Money can't buy happiness.* This reminds people that money is not an ultimate value although it often is treated as one. The saying may be used as a comment when a wealthy but lonely and wretched[3] person commits suicide.

Money, like love and sex, is so important to Americans because it relates so closely to the

---

[3] **Wretched** – deeply unhappy

three key values of success, self-esteem and fun. Money is a symbol of success and it can buy many other symbols. My self-esteem, as well as other people's view of me, will automatically go up if I have more money. Money buys the ticket to all kinds of fun. With money a person can reach all three main goals of American culture.

On the other hand, we say, *Money can't buy happiness.* We know this is true. We know some wealthy people are miserable. Their misery tells us that there must be more to life than success, self-esteem and fun, and yet many of us still chase money anyway. We speak of "the almighty dollar" as if money were God. For many Americans it is God. Some of us worship it, we make any sacrifice to get it, we hold it dearly and protect it zealously.[4] Getting money is the center of life. It affects everything.

As we will see later, we have got used to thinking that *Time is money (86).* We think we should work longer hours in order to get more money, even though this reduces the amount of time we have for pleasure and family. When we say *Time is money*, we are almost saying, "Life is money" (though there is no such proverb).

## Ask your American friends

### Opinions and experiences

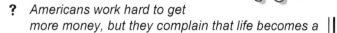

? *Americans work hard to get more money, but they complain that life becomes a* ||

---

[4] **Zealously** – eagerly and fiercely

*"rat race"[5] and everyone is too busy to enjoy it. Why don't more Americans take life a little easier and settle for less money?*

**?** *Suppose a good fairy[6] offered you this choice—for the rest of your life you can have all the love you need or all the money you need. What would you say?*

## Other proverbs to discuss
*(share some about your own country too)*

~ *Beggars can't be choosers.*

~ *The grass is always greener on the other side of the fence.*

~ *Keeping up with the Joneses.*

~ *If you're so smart, why ain't[7] you rich?*

~ *Money isn't everything.*

~ *The love of money is the root of all evil.*

~ *A fool and his money are soon parted.*

## PLAYING TO WIN

**32.** *We're number one.* This phrase means, "We are the best." It is often chanted[8] by the supporters of a sports team that has won a championship.

**33.** *Nice guys finish last.* If you are kind to your opponents, you will finish in last place in the contest. If

---

[5] **"Rat race"** – a meaningless but frantic competition

[6] **Good fairy** – an imaginary being in children's stories

[7] **Ain't** – slang for "aren't"

[8] **Chanted** – shouted in rhythm together

you want to win, sometimes you may have to be
unkind and impolite.

American play tends to be achievement-
oriented and competitive.[9] For example, in
Europe when people go hiking, most do it
primarily to enjoy the walk or the hike.
Americans do it because we want to conquer
something or prove something that will build
our self-esteem. Yes, we do have a bit of fun
looking at nature as we hike, but a lot of the
fun is in the success.

The same desire to conquer in play is obvious in the video games that American children spend millions of hours with every
week. Even when we log onto the Internet,
we do it with a "play to win" mentality.

And we do love the Internet. We have to. It is
such an American thing. After all, it is in-
stant, it is always changing, it is free (or almost free), it is fun, it is highly individualistic,
it is private, it multiplies choices by the mil-
lion, it lets us shop from home and it never
threatens our self-esteem unless we have to
admit that we fell for an on-line scam.

### *Ask your American friends*

#### *Opinions and experiences*

**?**  *How competitive are you? What
do you love to win at?*

**?**  *What is a "good loser"? Should I try to be one?*

---

[9] **Competitive** – eager to show that one can win

---

*Other proverbs to discuss*
*(share some about your own country too)*

~  *Winning isn't everything.*

~  *It isn't whether you win or lose, it's how you play the game.*

~  *The one who dies with the most toys wins.*

---

## LUST, GREED, AND VIOLENCE

34. *Fight fire with fire.* If someone is hitting you, hit him back. If someone is cheating you, cheat her. Do whatever it takes to teach evil people a lesson.

35. *An eye for an eye.* Similar to previous proverb. Justice is done by requiring evil people to suffer the same violence they used against others. If they have put out someone's eye, they should have an eye put out. (This is not followed literally in America. The constitution protects all Americans from "cruel and unusual punishment." But the principle still stands, "Let the punishment fit the crime.")

Americans think that the desire for love/sex, money, and winning are healthy things; however, if the desires are uncontrolled they can change into unhealthy desires—lust, greed, and violence. Americans do not agree about how far the healthy desires can go before they become unhealthy.

No common proverbs praise lust or greed, but the movies and the music industry feed lust and profit from it. The stock market and the gambling industry do the same with greed.

Violent video games, movies, and TV shows are far more popular than our proverbs would lead us to expect. A few well-known proverbs do justify violence. For example, we say, *Fight fire with fire,* that is, fight evil violence with good violence. We also say, *An eye for an eye*, or, *Enough is enough* (68).

The interesting thing is that the proverbs only justify violence as a defense, never as a way of winning. If violence is used to dominate another person or group, it not excused. It is called abuse or crime. The violent massacres at schools or movie theaters are called insane, though sometimes we wonder why they happen more in America than in other countries.

---

## *Ask your American friends*

### *Opinions and experiences*

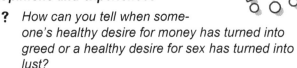

**?**   *How can you tell when some-one's healthy desire for money has turned into greed or a healthy desire for sex has turned into lust?*

**?**   *If your friend has a 10-year-old son who spends a lot of time playing violent adult video games, does your friend have anything to worry about? Why or why not?*

### *Movies to watch and discuss*

*The Searchers* (1956 classic Western with John Wayne). The hero, an ex-soldier of the Civil War, goes on a multi-year chase to find and rescue his niece after she is kidnapped by Native Americans.

Other options: *Raging Bull, Gone with the Wind, Wall Street, The Competition, Top Gun, Hoosiers*

Chapter Five

# Essentials for Achieving
# Any Goal

Americans assume two things about achieving any of our goals in life. First, each person must be free to pursue success. The purpose of government is to guarantee this freedom. Education and business are not supposed to create any barriers to this freedom. Second, each person must take initiative to use that freedom. In other words, government, business and education give us opportunities, but we have to make successes of ourselves.

## FREEDOM—EQUAL OPPORTUNITY FOR ALL

36. *Life, liberty and the pursuit of happiness.* These three "inalienable[1] rights" of human beings were emphasized in the American Declaration of Independence in 1776. Liberty is the freedom to hold personal opinions, make personal choices and take part as the community elects its leaders and makes its choices.

37. *The land of the free and the home of the brave.* This concluding line from the national anthem reminds Americans of freedom as our hallmark and bravery in war as the price of that freedom. The anthem was written after a battle in the War

---

[1] **Inalienable** – something that no one can take away

of 1812, when America defeated a British attempt to re-establish imperial control.

**38.** *We shall overcome.* This phrase is the title of a song which became a theme for African-Americans during the civil rights movement[2] of the 1960s. It referred to overcoming discrimination[3] and winning genuine freedom for minorities in America.

The "American Dream" of individual success depends on freedom for each and every citizen. When African-Americans, women, and other groups object to discrimination in education, housing, or employment, they are saying they have as much right to pursue the American Dream as anyone else does.

We claim that in America "all men are created equal" but we often treat minorities as "second-class citizens" and block their road to success. The civil rights movement and more recently the women's movement have pointed straight at the problem in many places. They sang, *We Shall Overcome*, and they did overcome much of the discrimination in laws, policies, and personal behavior.

These protest movements were not challenging the core values of American culture. On the contrary, they were affirming them. Protesters were demanding the freedom to make successes of themselves. They were protesting

---

[2] **Civil rights movement** – a citizens' campaign that changed many American laws and customs affecting ethnic minorities

[3] **Discrimination** – unfair treatment based on race or gender

a system that did not reward their hard work fairly.

The American reaction to the attacks on September 11, 2001, shows that we believe they were intolerable attacks on our freedom. We will not feel "free" if we have to wonder when the next plane will fly into a skyscraper and kill thousands more Americans. As a nation we will do whatever it takes to prevent that.

We Americans have our personal goals and we insist on being free to pursue them. No attack by a foreign enemy or discrimination by anyone in our own country can be allowed to interfere in "the land of the free."

---

### *Ask your American friends*

#### *Opinions and experiences*

**?**   *Do you think women and minorities are just as free as anyone else to succeed in America today? Can you give me some examples showing why you think so?*

**?**   *Do you think America will be as free in 20 or 30 years as it is now? What would keep it free? What would reduce its freedom?*

**?**   *Suppose you hear someone say, "Our huge military budget is not really protecting American freedom. It is getting us into expensive trouble all over the world. We should cut our budget and stay out of that trouble." Do you know anybody who thinks that? Would you agree or disagree with that person?*

## PERSONAL INITIATIVE

Freedom is like a sports field. It has been cleared of other obstacles and activities so that people can play on it. But freedom can remain unused, just as a sports field can. By itself, freedom does not make anyone a success. Many American proverbs encourage people to take some initiative and use their freedom. In fact, there are so many proverbs about initiative that we have to break them into groups to deal with them.

### *Doing something is better than doing nothing.*

39.   (Commandment 5) Just do it. This proverb is actually a recently invented advertising slogan[4] for the Nike shoe company. It may also be the best three-word summary of American cultural values. It means, "Quit being indecisive. Don't bother consulting a lot of people. Don't waste much time on planning. Just do it and do it now. It will be OK. If not, you can always fix it later, or leave it for someone else to deal with."

40. *The best defense is a good offense.* Be pro-active[5] and goal-oriented, not timid or conservative. Aim to conquer, not merely to protect yourself.

Americans are doers, which means we achieve a lot in life. We do not accept bad situations

---

[4] **Slogan** – a short statement describing a core value

[5] **Pro-active** – ready to take action before the situation forces you to

as inevitable. We try to do something about them. We protest. We fix. We invent. We improve. We believe progress is possible and any individual can make it. We work hard without giving up, and we often succeed.

On the other hand, *Just do it* (39) is extremely bad advice in many other cultures. Americans who operate that way are very offensive when visiting other countries. Americans get a reputation for being impatient and inconsiderate. We do not consult the people who should be consulted before action is taken. We ask directly for whatever we want.

---

## *Ask your American friends*

### *Opinions and experiences*

**?**  *Do you support any causes that involve fixing something that is wrong with the community, the nation, or the world? If so, how did you get interested and what are you doing to support the cause?*

### *Other proverbs to discuss*
*(share some about your own country too)*

~   *Talk is cheap.*
~   *Put your money where your mouth is.*
~   *Actions speak louder than words.*
~   *Never put off till tomorrow what you can do today.*
~   *The road to hell is paved with good intentions.*
~   *Idle hands are the devil's workshop.*

**See also**: *Opportunity only knocks once (88).*

### Depending on yourself and your own initiative

**41.** *Stand on your own two feet.* Grow up; act like an adult. Don't ask me to do something for you. This may be said to a young or immature[6] person who depends too much on others. It is like a cow kicking a grown calf that still wants to suckle.

**42.** *If you want something done right, do it yourself.* This discourages people from trusting anyone except themselves. It may be said to someone who asks another person to do a job for him or her and then complains about how it was done.

**43.** *There is no harm in trying.* A person expects to be respected for making an effort even if it does not succeed. This view encourages people to take risks.

**44.** *No pain no gain.* One must put forth an effort in order to succeed. (This saying comes from physical fitness instructors. They say that if you do not exercise hard enough to make your muscles hurt, the exercise is not doing you much good.)

In America growing up means becoming independent, *standing on your own two feet (41).* Children are dependent on others. Adults are seen as independent and self-sufficient. This contrasts sharply with many traditional cultures where growing up means becoming inter-dependent with other adults. In those cultures the main questions in life are, "Whom can I depend on?" and "Who can depend on me?" Americans do not take those questions very seriously. We just assume it is safer to depend on ourselves.

---

[6] **Immature** – not yet acting like an adult

Americans believe success is better than failure but failure is better than not trying. When we fail we say, "At least I tried." We expect people to respect us for trying. We think they will forgive us easily if we tried in a wrong way as long as our intentions were good.

We do not expect this independent kind of life to be easy, but we say, *No pain, no gain (44).* We are willing to go through some pain in order to achieve our goals. We look down on people who set no goals and only look for the easiest way to get through life.

## Ask your American friends

### Opinions and experiences

**?**  *You say,* If you want something done right, do it yourself. *In some countries people would rather say, "If you want something done right, get some friends to help you." What do you think of that idea?*

**?**  *In many countries it is a great disgrace to fail, so we do not try things unless we are fairly sure we can succeed. But in America, you seem to try anything. Do you really think it is better to fail at something than not to try it?*

### Other proverbs to discuss
*(share some about your own country too)*

~  *You've got to take the bull by the horns.*

~  *Money doesn't grow on trees.*

~  *Necessity is the mother of invention.*

~ *Too many cooks spoil the broth.*

~ *Easy come, easy go.*

~ *Nothing ventured, nothing gained.*

~ *First come, first served.*

### Knowing the proper limits of initiative

45. *Give him an inch and he'll take a mile.* Be careful of presumptuous[7] people who take more initiative than they should. If you do someone a small favor or delegate a little power to them, they may take advantage of you.

46. *If it ain't broke, don't fix it.* Do not bother trying to improve something if it is already working satisfactorily. That is a waste of time and you run the risk of breaking the thing while you are trying to improve it.

47. *All things come to him who waits.* Sometimes patience is better than initiative.

In most cases Americans like initiative but not always. These proverbs warn us about initiative of certain kinds.

Sometimes it is better to leave things alone than to try to improve them. Sometimes humility and patience may be the best route to success. However, we see these warnings as exceptions. In most cases we would rather take charge and try to make things happen as we want.

---

[7] **Presumptuous** – acting as if you have more permission than you have really been given

## Ask your American friends

**?**  *Americans say,* All things come to him who waits. *Can you give an example of a time when you decided to wait for something to happen instead of trying to make it happen quickly, and your patience paid off?*

### Other proverbs about limits to initiative

~  *Fools rush in where angels fear to tread.*

~  *Leave well enough alone.*

~  *The cure is worse than the disease.*

~  *Count to ten before you lose your temper.*

**See also**: *Let a sleeping dog lie (80).*

### Movies to watch and discuss:

*Finding Nemo* (2003 animated comedy-drama, G). A young fish ignores his father's warnings about the open ocean and is caught up in a string of adventures, including losing and regaining his freedom.

Other options: *To Kill a Mockingbird, The Wizard of Oz, All the President's Men, The Insiders*

## Chapter Six

# Age, Gender, and Human Nature

## AGE

**48.** *(Commandment 6) You are only young once.* Do what you can while you are young. For example, go to Europe for a couple months during your summer break from college. Once you graduate from college and begin your adult working life, that opportunity will be gone.

**49.** *A man is only as old as he feels.* A person's energy level is more important than age.

**50.** *Oh, for the vigor[1] of youth again.* An expression used sadly by a middle-aged or older person, often when observing a child or youth doing something very active.

From an American point of view, youth is the ideal time of life. It is the time of the most freedom, the most choices, the most vitality and the fewest obligations. Middle age and old age are a long, losing battle to stay young, look young and feel young. Aging is seen only as a loss of liveliness and strength, not an increase in prestige[2] or wisdom.

---

[1] **Vigor** – energy and strength.

[2] **Prestige** – high status in the eyes of others

Retirement, usually beginning at age 65, is seen as a time of self-indulgence. Many retirees move south to Florida or Arizona because the weather is warmer, even though this means moving far away from relatives and friends.

People from other cultures may wonder whether retired Americans have any sense that they are worth anything as human beings. They are hundreds or thousands of miles from their children. No one shows them any special respect. But they still have their self-esteem. They may regard retirement itself as an achievement, perhaps the one great success to which the rest of life was looking forward. A retiree may say, "I worked all my life for it. I made money and saved money. Now I am free to have fun."

One of the most important differences between American culture and many others is that in America one's sense of worth comes more from personal achievements than from relationships. A great deal of American culture will not make sense to the outsider until this point is recognized.

## Ask your American friends

### Opinions and experiences

**?** *Tell me about your oldest living relatives (parents or grandparents). What are their lives like, where do they live, is anybody taking care of them, etc.?*

> **?** *Do you see anything good about getting old? Do Americans get more respect and honor as they get older or not?*
>
> **?** *Do you agree that "one's sense of worth comes more from personal achievements than from relationships"? Who or what makes you feel valuable?*

## GENDER

**51.** *A man's home is his castle.* At home a man is like a king, completely free to do as he wishes.

**52.** *A man may work from sun to sun, but woman's work is never done.* Men may have to work long days but they can go home to rest in the evening. Women (working in the home or at an outside job or both) can never get away from what used to be called "woman's work," such as cooking and cleaning.

**53.** *Celebrate diversity.* A recent slogan intended to promote acceptance of people different from oneself. It is often used by the homosexual community. In that case it means, "Do not criticize anyone because of his or her sexual orientation.[3] Instead accept and even celebrate the fact that people have different likes and dislikes in sexual activity as in other aspects of life."

The definitions of male and female roles in American society are under fierce debate in America today. What makes a man masculine? What makes a woman feminine? How can a woman be fulfilled as a housewife if there is no obvious personal achievement

---

[3] **Sexual orientation** – one's preference for having sex with the opposite sex, the same sex or both

and no pay? Is sexual orientation purely a matter of personal preference?

Because Americans are so divided about gender issues, most of the above proverbs about gender will offend somebody. For example, feminists are offended by sayings like, *A man's home is his castle (51)*, or *Woman's work is never done (52)*. They believe these are old-fashioned, oppressive ideas.

Traditionalists, on the other hand, are deeply offended when homosexuals adopt the new slogan, *Celebrate diversity (53)*. Traditionalists see homosexuality as perversity,[4] not just diversity, and they do not want anyone to celebrate perversity.

## Ask your American friends

### Opinions and experiences

**?** *What do you think of when you hear the slogan,* Celebrate diversity*? How far do you agree with that idea?*

**?** *Do women have a different place in American society than they did ten or twenty years ago? What has changed and what else still needs to change (if anything)?*

### Other proverbs to discuss
*(share some about your own country too)*

---

[4] **Perversity** – gross immorality; human beings acting like animals

~  *It's a woman's prerogative[5] to change her mind.*

~  *Clothes make the man.*

~  *Beauty is only skin deep.*

## HUMAN NATURE

54. *Nobody is perfect.* Everyone has shortcomings. This is used as an excuse for a minor mistake that has been made.

55. *Boys will be boys.* People will act according to their nature, including some mischief.[6] This is sometimes used to describe irresponsible but not too seriously wrong behavior by men. In other words, grown men will sometimes act like little boys.

56. *One bad apple can spoil the whole barrel.* Do not associate with bad people. They may spoil you as a rotting apple spoils the apples next to it in the barrel.

Americans recognize that all human beings have faults. *Nobody is perfect (54).* We can keep a healthy self-esteem without thinking we are perfect. But we could not keep it if we thought we were basically evil.

We tend to think that only a very few people are really bad people. They are the "bad apples" *(56)* who influence ordinary people to

do bad things. They deliberately harm people and may even enjoy watching others suffer.

---

[5] **Prerogative** – a right that cannot be questioned

[6] **Mischief** – behavior that is wrong but not very serious

The rest of us don't do that so we don't see ourselves as evil.

If we happen to hurt someone while we are only intending to protect ourselves, we call that "self-preservation" or *"Looking out for number one" (19)*. If we do something and someone is offended by it, we may excuse ourselves by saying, "That's just the way I am," or *Boys will be boys (55)*. We call this "self-expression."

This may not make much sense to foreigners. Americans consider selfishness to be very bad but self-interest (including self-esteem, self-sufficiency, self-preservation and self-expression) to be very good.

---

### *Ask your American friends*

#### *Opinions and experiences*

**?** *Americans seem to see a big difference between selfishness and self-interest, but aren't those two things very similar? What do you think the difference is?*

**?** *Would you agree that most Americans are basically good people even though they are basically focused on themselves? In other words, they can be "good" without being focused on others more than on themselves.*

#### *Other proverbs to discuss*
*(share some about your own country too)*

~ *To err is human.*

~ *When the cat's away the mice will play.*

~ *Better the devil you know than the devil you don't.*

## Movies to watch and discuss

*Cocoon* (1985 sci-fi, PG-13). A group of retired people discover a new life-force that aliens, who are disguised as humans, have put into a private swimming pool.

Other options: *Up, The Bucket List, City Slickers, Tootsie, A League of Their Own, Ma Vie en Rose, Some Like it Hot*

## Chapter Seven

# Loyalties, Groups and Families

### LOYALTIES

57. *If you scratch my back, I'll scratch yours.* If you do a favor for me, I will do one for you. (This refers to a pleasurable back-scratch, not an attack from behind.)

58. *A friend in need is a friend indeed.* My true friend is the one who shows loyalty to me by helping me when I am in need.

59. *Rats desert a sinking ship.* A losing cause is abandoned. This is generally used to criticize the people who are abandoning a project that appears to be failing, since they are compared to rats.

60. *A good captain goes down with his ship.* Contrast to previous proverb. The captain remains on board his ship even when all hope to save it is lost.

As we have seen in various other sections of this book, Americans' primary loyalty is to ourselves as individuals. The proverb *Looking out for number one (19)* sums up this view. All other duties and loyalties have to be seen in light of this basic loyalty to self.

This means that a person's loyalty can never be assumed. It must be earned by continually showing the person that he or she will be better off by remaining loyal. For example, a sports team that wants loyal fans[1] must keep winning. Even marriage partners may feel they have to keep earning each other's loyalty.

Loyalty may break down if a cause seems lost. *Rats desert a sinking ship (59),* that is, saving one's own life is more important than the welfare of the cause or the group. On the other hand, we also say, *A good captain goes down with his ship (60).* He is so loyal to the ship that if she ever begins to sink, he does everything he can to save her and everyone on board. He may even give up his life as he is doing his duty.

We admire that kind of heroic loyalty, but we rarely see it or do it. Loyalty to companies, to neighborhoods and even to friends seems to mean less than it used to. Loyalty puts limits on our freedom to choose, and we generally do not like those limits.

## *Ask your American friends*

### *Opinions and experiences*

? *What loyalties do you have besides loyalty to yourself? How much have those loyalties been tested?*

? *Is there any person or group of people you expect to be loyal to you for your whole life, no matter what happens? Why will they be loyal?*

### *Other proverbs to discuss*
*(share some about your own country too)*

~ *One good turn deserves another.*

---

[1] **Fans** – supporters of a team

~   *A live dog is better than a dead lion.*

~   *My country, right or wrong.*

~   *Blood is thicker than water.*

~   *No man can serve two masters.*

~   *A dog is a man's best friend.*

## GROUPS

**61.** *Birds of a feather flock together.* People with similar characteristics and interests will spend their time together. This may be used as a warning against associating with bad people. Others will assume one is like them.

**62.** *There is safety in numbers.* Do not take large risks all by yourself. Do not walk alone on a dangerous street at night.

**63.** *Many hands make light work.* Cooperation makes a job much easier.

**64.** *Misery loves company.* When things go badly, a person wants a group of friends to share the pain. This can also mean that when people are miserable, they may want to make others miserable too. Such people are dangerous.

One might suppose that Americans are so individualistic that we have little use at all for belonging to any group. This is not quite true. We have already seen that belonging to a group can make fun more enjoyable and success more likely. *Many hands make light work (63).*

Belonging to a group may also be important because of shared interests *(Birds of a feath-*

*er flock together, 61),* safety *(There is safety in numbers, 62),* and sympathy *(Misery loves company, 64).*

Americans do not mind group relationships. What bothers us is group obligations.[2] We join groups easily and we leave groups easily. In other words, we join groups which serve our personal interests and we remain with a group for as long as we wish to enjoy it, but no longer. Americans' ease with group relationships makes it easy for us to engage in conversation or form casual friendships with complete strangers but very hard for us to form deep and lasting relationships. Personal freedom or self-development is rarely sacrificed for the sake of a group.

Facebook is an example of an ideal group with no obligations. The user can continually decide whether to open Facebook or not and whether to post anything or not. It is available whenever the user wants it but there are no penalties for failing to check it for a week or a month. The old news is simply pushed down the list and out of view by the new news.

Texting is more complex. On one hand, it is desired because (unlike the phone) it puts minimum obligation on the recipient. It barely interrupts the recipients. It does not require them to participate in greetings or any

---

[2] **Obligations** – what the group expects or requires of all members

other small talk or to respond with more than "OK" or "LOL."

On the other hand, texting is a social power tool. It defines an inner circle of friends (an in-group). The group can become so interlocked that they can barely sit down to lunch without texting to find out what the others are doing at that moment. The members do have an endless obligation to notice and respond to texts from other members. Otherwise they get cut off from the list of text recipients.

America is in transition in this matter of belonging to groups. There is a very widespread longing for relationships that are "meaningful" or "authentic," the kind of relationships associated with group activities and small-town America in the past, yet Americans do not want to go back to the past.

Neither do we want any cuts in our standard of living even though our high standard makes it hard for us to develop any group solidarity.[3] The American way of life is set up to prevent difficult times or to allow us to deal with them as individuals when they come. But this also prevents us from developing strong bonds in our groups. We never find out who our real friends are because

---

[3] **Solidarity** – a strong feeling of belonging; willingness to sacrifice for the benefit of the group

we never get to see who would step up to help us if we really needed it.

## Ask your American friends

### Opinions and experiences

**?** Do you agree that "Americans enjoy groups but don't like group obligations"? What kind of group obligations are Americans OK with? Why?

**?** What groups do you belong to that are an important part of your life? How long have you belonged to them?

**?** How hard would it be for you to give up texting for a week? Is there any group that would wonder what had happened to you?

### Other proverbs to discuss
(share some about your own country too)

~ Two heads are better than one.

~ A house divided against itself cannot stand.

~ Two is company and three is a crowd.

**See also:** One bad apple can spoil the whole barrel (56).

### THE FAMILY AS A GROUP

65. *Charity begins at home.* One should be kind to close relatives before doing good to the community in general.

66. *Home, sweet home.* Traditionally used on plaques hung on the wall, this phrase reminds people of the ideal home. It should be a place of warmth, love and joy. The phrase may be used by people returning home at the end of a long trip.

**67.** *Home is where the heart is.* Home is wherever
ones loved ones are. The size or appearance of
a house does not make it a home or keep it from
being a home.

The very first point to recognize in a discussion of American families is that Americans
apply the word "family" almost entirely to the
"nuclear family"[4] not to the "extended family"
as in most other cultures. Many Americans
live hundreds or thousands of miles from their
nearest "extended family" relative. Contacts
with aunts, uncles and cousins are often lost.
Many of us do not have any one city we really
call "home." We do not have a family cemetery.[5] Our parents or grandparents do not live
in our home.

The proverbs about home reflect the era of
my parents' childhood much more than the
situation today. *Home, sweet home (66)*
sounds like wishful thinking to a lot of us
today. Things are different now. Home is not
where the heart is. Home is where the televi-
sion is (though again, we have no proverb
that says so, and most Americans may laugh
at that phrase.)

Everything about American homes is moving
toward greater individualism. Each family
member goes off to her own room and her

[4] **Nuclear family** – only parents and children living together
while the children grow up. The "extended family" means
other relatives such as grandparents, adult brothers and sis-
ters, cousins, etc.

[5] **Cemetery** – place where the dead are buried

own TV or computer. The microwave oven splits up the family so a family rarely eats a meal at the same time.

There is much talk in America about a recovery of "family values."[6] A popular religious movement in the 90s called "Promise Keepers" filled football stadiums nationwide for weekend all-male conferences. Men were urged to keep their promises to wives, children and God. The problem with such a campaign is that just like other loyalties and group relationships, "family values" put limits on individual choices and freedoms. Not all Americans want to pay that price in order to improve family relationships.

If we want to recover strong family relationships, our proverbs will not help us much. There are no common American proverbs specifically about being a good parent, husband, wife or child, or about showing special respect to a person in any of these roles.

## Ask your American friends

### Opinions and experiences

**?**  *What do you think "American family values" are? Should America go back to them?*

**?**  *How many cousins, aunts and uncles do you have? When did you last see them?*

**?**  *When do American families talk to each other? For example, when I see a family in a restaurant, each*

---

[6] **Family values** – beliefs that emphasize the importance of family relationships

*person seems to be texting or playing a video game instead of talking.*

## Other proverbs to discuss
*(share some about your own country too)*

~ *There is no place like home.*

~ *Baseball, motherhood and apple pie.*

~ *Like father, like son.*

~ *Spare the rod and spoil the child.*

## Movies to watch and discuss

*E.T. the Extra-Terrestrial* (1982 sci-fi, PG).
A dysfunctional[7] family is gradually drawn back together as they collaborate to protect an alien from other humans until his family (who fled and left him behind) can return to rescue him.

Other options: *Toy Story (1, 2, or 3), Mrs. Doubtfire, It's a Wonderful Life, The Godfather, The Notebook, Ordinary People, 50 First Dates, Juno, Radio Days*

---

[7] **Dysfunctional** – not working well, not able to work together

## Chapter Eight

# Fairness, Blame and Conflict

## JUSTICE AND FAIRNESS

In any culture which places such a high value on individual success won by strategy, hard work and wise risk-taking, one has to ask what is considered fair. Are there any moral limits to strategy? How are success and freedom limited by justice?

68. *(Commandment 7) Enough is enough.* This very common proverb means, "I have had enough of the unjust things you are doing to me or to the ones I love. I am not going to take it any more. I am going to act to put some justice into this situation." Americans highly respect people who stand up for their rights and change a bad or unjust situation.

69. *What goes around comes around.* What you do to others, especially if it is bad, will eventually be done to you. As you seek your own success, do not treat other people badly. They may take revenge[1] and spoil your success.

70. *Do unto others as you would have them do to you.* Similar to previous proverb (which could be phrased, "Do not do to others what you do not want them to do back to you.") The "Do unto others . . ." form is the "Golden Rule" from the Bible. It is not a warning but a command—treat others justly.

---

[1] **Take revenge** – try to get even. Attack the one who attacked you.

**71.** *Innocent until proven guilty.* In a court of law, the accused person is presumed innocent at the start. The burden of proof[2] always rests on the accuser, not the accused. The jury will not convict the person unless the proof is clear.

Human rights are the standard of American justice. Whatever protects human rights is just; whatever goes against human rights is unjust. Every American of whatever status has many personal rights, guaranteed by the "Bill of Rights" in the Constitution. These include such things as the right to speak one's mind in public (even if this insults the government), the right to worship as one pleases and the right to trial by a jury of fellow citizens.

When people's rights are violated,[3] they are expected to react strongly enough to stop the injustice. Sometimes it may also be considered fair for them to require some payment for the injustice that was done to them or even to inflict a punishment. *What goes around comes around (69).*

Since Americans believe that all human beings have the right to be treated fairly, we will not let anyone treat us unfairly. Such treatment shows that the person thinks we are slaves, animals or some other thing that is less than a human being. We will not stand for it.

---

[2] **Burden of proof** – responsibility to prove something

[3] **Violated** – broken without a legal reason

## Ask your American friends
### Opinions and experiences

**?** *When did something bother you so
much that you said to yourself,
"Enough is enough"? What did you do to change it?*

### Other proverbs to discuss
*(share some about your own country too)*

~ *Silence is consent.*

~ *Turnabout is fair play.*

~ *Honesty is the best policy.*

~ *Justice is blind.*

~ *Finders keepers, losers weepers.*

~ *Possession is nine-tenths of the law*

**See also:** *If you scratch my back, I'll scratch yours
(57); Don't get mad, get even (84).*

### BLAME

72. *The devil made me do it.* I am not to blame for
    what I did. I could not help it. Some power out-
    side of me was forcing me to act in that way.

73. *If the shoe fits, wear it.* If an accusation is true,
    accept the blame. (This saying can also mean,
    "If a suitable opportunity comes to you, take it.")

74. *You made the bed, you lie in it.* You created a
    certain situation so you are now responsible to
    take the consequences.

75. *The pot calling the kettle[4] black.* Since the pot
    and the kettle are equally black from the cooking

---

[4] **Kettle** – a large old-fashioned cooking pot

fire, the pot has no right to criticize the kettle. This might be used if a person gossips[5] but also criticizes someone else for gossiping.

**76.** *Get a life.* Do not be so unreasonably critical about tiny things. Find something better to do with your time.

If we succeed at something, we want to take credit for it. If we fail, we want to find someone else to blame. We may playfully say, *"The devil made me do it (72)."* This is an excuse used by people who know they have done something wrong but want to avoid the penalty. It does not necessarily mean they really believe a devil exists or has any influence over their choices.

By passing the blame we try to protect our self-esteem. Several proverbs remind us that each individual really is responsible for her actions. *You made the bed, you lie in it (74).* Justice means that a person will have to pay for his crimes. No individual can escape this responsibility before the law of the land, regardless of personal status, wealth, or power.

Though we do not like to take responsibility for our own actions, we love to demand that other people take responsibility for theirs. If their action hurts us in any way, we make them pay. Americans sue[6] (and win) over matters that would get laughed out of court in most countries.

---

[5] **Gossips** – spreads stories, often not exactly true, that harm other people

[6] **Sue** (or "file suit") – go to court to accuse another person of harming you in some way and ask the court to force the person to pay for the harm done

## Ask your American friends

### Opinions and experiences

**?**   Why do Americans say, *"The devil made me do it,"* if they don't believe there is a devil?

**?**   What do you do to protect yourself from being sued? Have you ever had to sue a person or company? What was the problem?

### Other proverbs to discuss
*(share some about your own country too)*

~   *You can lead a horse to water, but you can't make him drink.*

~   *Crime does not pay.*

~   *Be sure your sins will find you out.*

~   *Chickens come home to roost.*

~   *There are two sides to every story.*

### AUTHORITIES AND RULES

When freedom of choice, self-expression, self-development, and self-esteem are core values in a culture, there is not much room left for authorities and rules. We have already seen several proverbs that imply that each individual is his or her own authority: *If it feels good, do it (22)*; *Just do it (39)*; *Live and let live* (18) and *The customer is always right* (20). There are also proverbs that directly mention authorities and rules.

**77.** (Commandment 8) *Rules are made to be broken.* Rules are not to be blindly and absolutely followed. Wise people will always ask themselves whether a rule really applies to their own circumstances. If it does not, they will break the rule in order to do what appears best at this particular time.

**78.** *The voice of the people is the voice of God.* The ultimate authority in a society is found in the consensus[7] of the average people.

**79.** *Power corrupts.* Do not trust a person who has been in power for very long. When people are put into positions of power, they gradually forget what life is like for ordinary people. They become more likely to abuse their power, perhaps without even realizing it.

In many cultures, proverbs remind people to trust and respect authorities of all kinds. By contrast, American proverbs teach people to question and challenge authorities. Our nation was born in a revolution that threw off an unwanted authority, and we have been throwing off authority ever since. Many of us do not want to deny all authority by saying, *If it feels good, do it (22).* Yet we each want to be our own authority with as little limitation as possible from other authorities in government, society, family and the workplace.

If an authority makes a demand on us, we want to know the reason. If the reason does not look obvious and necessary to us, we may say, *Rules are made to be broken (77).*

---

[7] **Consensus** – community agreement after discussion

For example, if a child asks a parent, "Why can't I do that?" and the parent replies, "Because I said so," the child does not accept this. If the parent gives no explanation, the child does not see any authority in the demand.

American skepticism[8] about authorities is also true of rules. Most Americans see rules as limits to freedom. The fewer rules the better.

In fact, we do not like to quote proverbs in a way that makes them sound like rules. Sometimes we may stand a proverb on its head[9] to show we do not accept it as a rule any more. For example, the old saying, *Crime doesn't pay* becomes *Crime pays*. Or we change *Flattery will get you nowhere* to *Flattery will get you everywhere*. The person who can question authority is more respected than the one who submits to authority without thinking.

---

## *Ask your American friends*

### *Opinions and experiences*

**?**  *If American children are taught to question every authority including parents and teachers, when and how do they learn to accept authority? How did you learn it?*

**?**  *Americans say,* Rules are made to be broken, *yet most of the time you obey rules. How do you decide which rules to keep and which ones it is OK to break?*

---

[8] **Skepticism** – doubt; unwillingness to trust

[9] **Stand a proverb on its head** – change a proverb to the opposite meaning

*Other proverbs to discuss*
(share some from your country too)

~  *There is an exception to every rule.*

~  *The exception proves the rule.*

~  *The devil can quote scripture.*

## CONFLICT AND RECONCILIATION

80. *Let a sleeping dog lie.* Do not meddle in something that will cause you no trouble if you leave it alone. If you wake up the "dog," it may bite you.

81. *If you can't stand the heat, get out of the kitchen.* Withdraw from an activity if you do not like the conflict and criticism it brings. Let other people do it without you.

82. *Two wrongs don't make a right.* If someone does a wrong to you, react with justice, not by doing something vicious. [10]

83. *He who laughs last, laughs best.* If a person does wrong to someone and laughs at him or her, the victim will look for a way to get revenge. When revenge is taken, the victim *gets the last laugh,* defeating the other person.

84. *Don't get mad, get even.* Similar to the previous proverb. When someone treats you badly, do not just get angry, express your anger in action.

85. *Let bygones[11] be bygones.* Do not bring up an old problem. Pretend it never happened.

---

[10] **Vicious** – intending to cause as much harm as possible

[11] **Bygones** – things that have "gone by," that is, things that are over and should be forgotten

Americans do not enjoy conflict for its own sake. The proverb, *Let a sleeping dog lie,* advises people to avoid conflict if possible. Americans tend to avoid discussion of religion and politics because they believe such discussion can easily lead to conflicts. (University students are less worried about this than other Americans.)

We do realize that some degree of conflict is normal in life and may even be healthy. It helps people learn how to stand up for themselves, which is very important in an individualistic society. But we are disturbed by the fact that conflict is getting more violent in our society.

For example, "road rage" is one of the most frightening new forms of violence. This term refers to one driver attacking or even killing another on the highway because of the way he was driving. The attacker thinks this way: "I am just as important as anyone on the road. That driver was treating me like a piece of dirt. I had to show him that he cannot get away with that. *Enough is enough*" (68).

Though Americans believe in protecting our personal dignity and we may say, *Don't get mad, get even,* we are not at all sympathetic[12] to this kind of violence. We don't want self-assertion to get out of hand. That is why *Live and let live* (Commandment 2) is such an important proverb for us. It sets

---

[12] **Sympathetic** – willing to understand

limits                                              on aggressiveness.[13] There is also a gentler side to American values that says, *Let bygones be bygones (85).*

## Ask your American friends

### Opinions and experiences

**?** *Do you generally avoid talking about religion and politics in order to avoid conflict with other people? Can you explain that for me? In many countries people love to argue about those things.*

**?** *How do you explain road rage? Does it indicate anything about America in general or is it only a few crazy people doing it?*

### Other proverbs to discuss
*(share some about your own country too)*

~ *It takes two to make a quarrel.*

~ *The pen is mightier than the sword.*

~ *People who live in glass houses should not throw stones.*

~ *Sticks and stones may break my bones but words will never hurt me.*

~ *Opposites attract.*

~ *Revenge is sweet.*

~ *Forgive and forget.*

~ *Time heals all wounds.*

---

[13] **Aggressiveness** – a tendency to force oneself on others

**See also:** *Boys will be boys (55).*

## *Movies to watch and discuss*

*Cool Hand Luke* (1967, drama). A man imprisoned for a very small crime refuses to submit to either the prison officials or the dominant inmates. Whether he wins or loses, he fights everything that looks unfair to him.

Other options: *One Flew Over the Cuckoo's Nest, M.A.S.H., Smokey and the Bandit, To Kill a Mockingbird, Seven Pounds, Avatar, The Apartment, Social Network*

**Chapter Nine**

# Time and Change

If you get the impression that Americans are always in a hurry, you are right. Americans look at time as a scarce, valuable thing. There may be more American sayings about time than any other subject, and they are probably the sayings you will hear the most.

86. *(Commandment 9) Time is money.* Time can be converted to money, that is, wages are often paid per hour of work. Managers want employees to do things quickly because "time is money." If employees waste time, the company loses money.

87. *Making every minute count.* Doing something productive all the time. Not letting any time slip away.

88. *Opportunity only knocks once.* Similar to previous two proverbs. Opportunity is like an unexpected stranger passing by. It knocks on someone's door. If the person fails to answer the door, opportunity goes away and knocks on someone else's door. It does not return to the same person.

89. *The sooner the better.* A wish for quick action or quick change. Once a decision has been made, there is no point in waiting to carry it out.

90. *Make it short and sweet.* Speak briefly and to the point. We do not have time for the details.

In chapter 4 we noted the connection between time and money. Life is seen as an hourglass in which the days slip by like grains of sand until one's time is up. Life is

not seen as an accumulation,[1] an unfolding, a growth. It is a race, a race against time, and the human being always loses.

What is true of a lifetime is also true of each day, hour and minute. Americans are time-conscious to an extreme. Next to the credit card, the clock is our worst slave driver.[2] This view of time accounts for the very high level of stress in American life today.

Since time is limited and lost opportunities are gone forever, one has to go through life *making every minute count (87).* That means one is always busy doing something (work or play) or experiencing something.

We schedule everything, including our play. Then we say our schedules are so full that we need a vacation, but even on a "vacation" we try to pack in as many experiences as we can. We joke about getting home and having to recover from our vacation.

Time spent sitting and reflecting does not count for much. It doesn't make any money. It doesn't "do" anything. In fact, silence makes Americans nervous, as if we think time is being wasted or boredom is on the way. We try to fill up the silence, perhaps by turning on a TV or radio just to have some noise in the background.

---

[1] **Accumulation** – something that gradually collects

[2] **Slave driver** – a thing or person that forces us to do what we do not want to do, as if we were slaves

## Ask your American friends

### Opinions and experiences

**?** *Americans seem to be obsessed with time, making every minute count. How does that attitude improve the quality of life and how does it reduce it?*

**?** *Do most Americans think they are too busy? If so, how did they get that way? Why do they stay that way? What is pushing them?*

**?** *My book says that Americans do not think that sitting and reflecting on life is very important. Do you agree? When do you sit in silence and reflect? What do you think about?*

### Other proverbs to discuss
(share some from your country too)

~ *Time's a-wasting.*

~ *Time flies.*

~ *No time like the present.*

~ *Now or never.*

~ *Make hay while the sun shines.*

~ *He who hesitates is lost.*

~ *Business and pleasure don't mix.*

~ *The early bird catches the worm.*

~ *Early to bed and early to rise makes a man healthy, wealthy and wise.*

~ *Haste makes waste.*

~ *Better late than never.*

**See also:** *You are only young once (48).*

## CHANGE AND PROGRESS

**91.** *Time marches on.* Time is marching to its own drumbeat. It does not slow down or stop for anyone.

**92.** *A new broom sweeps clean.* A new person in power will change many things and improve the situation. Change is better than leaving things as they are.

**93.** *Tomorrow is another day,* (or, *Tomorrow is a new day.*) No matter how bad things are right now, a person may hope for better prospects in the morning. New opportunities will come.

**94.** *History repeats itself.* There are patterns in history. Nations rise and fall for similar reasons. Nations do not change their ways or learn from the mistakes of others. They repeat them.

We live in a society where everything can change, and almost everything does. There are new styles of clothing, new hit songs, maybe a new job or even a new spouse. We elect a new president. We open a new highway, a new mall and a new housing development. We expect all this change as *Time marches on (91).*

Many changeless traditions common in other countries are not found in America at all. There is no American national costume, no definitive American folk tales or myths, no folk songs that everyone knows and no standard American way to conduct weddings or funerals. We do not even have an official national language.

We welcome change because we have a deep belief that *Tomorrow is another day (93),* and things are going to get better. Someone will find a cure for AIDS, a cheaper alternative for gasoline or a diet pill[3] that works. The human beings of the future will be stronger, smarter, and happier than people today.

What is the basis for our faith in progress? Historically it has been faith in individual hard work and bright ideas, especially in the areas of science and technology. For example, we point to the computer as an idea that has brought huge changes, mostly good, to many parts of life.

Much as we like change, we know that some things are almost impossible to change. For example, we doubt that our government will ever do anything efficiently. Government is by nature bureaucratic,[4] monopolistic[5] and non-profit. Nevertheless, we keep trying to "change the system," "re-invent government," etc. We try for small changes even when we despair about any big changes.

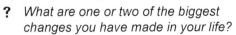

## *Ask your American friends*

### *Opinions and experiences*

**?** *What are one or two of the biggest changes you have made in your life?*

**?** *My country has lots of traditions and they give our lives meaning. Traditions do not seem to be very important in America, and I don't quite understand*

---

[3] **Diet pill** – a pill that causes a person to lose weight

[4] **Bureaucratic** – organized in a very structured way

[5] **Monopolistic** – not allowing any competition

*where American life gets its meaning or its stability without them. Can you help me?*

**?** *Is the world generally changing for the better or going downhill?⁶ Will technology make life much better for most people in the next generation?*

**?** *You say, "History repeats itself." Does that mean it is a waste of time to try to change things? Is there any way to break the cycle of history repeating itself?*

### Other proverbs to discuss
(share some from your country too)

~ *The worm turns.*

~ *Here today, gone tomorrow.*

~ *The darkest hour is just before the dawn.*

~ *Will wonders never cease?*

~ *You can't teach an old dog new tricks.*

~ *The more things change, the more they stay the same.*

~ *Nature abhors a vacuum.*

~ *The leopard cannot change his spots.*

**See also:** *Time and tide wait for no man (100).*

### Movies to watch and discuss
*The Right Stuff* (1983, drama, action and adventure, PG). The story of the test pilots and astronauts who pushed the boundaries of technology in the "space race" of the 1950s and early 60s.

Other options: *Far and Away, Wall-E, Star Trek (any movie or TV show in the series), Outbreak, The Village, Modern Times, 20,000 Leagues Under the Sea*

---

⁶ **Going downhill** – getting worse

Chapter Ten

# Hope and God

## OPTIMISM

In chapter 2 on success we saw that Americans take risks confidently and work with determination in spite of setbacks. In chapter 9 we saw the American belief that changes are usually improvements. This optimism is also clear in the following more general proverbs.

**95.** *Look on the bright side.* Try to see the good side of a difficult situation. Keep your hopes up.

**96.** *Half a loaf is better than no bread at all.* Sometimes we will not be able to get all we want or hope for. At such times of only partial success, we should be glad for what we do get.

These proverbs represent an underlying American cultural belief that we should be positive about life, even the parts of life that seem difficult. If we *look on the bright side (95)*, we are more likely to keep trying for success. Though we never like to settle for a partial success, *Half a loaf is better than no bread at all (96)*. Perhaps we can get the other half of the loaf later. We have almost limitless faith in our own ability to change things for the better.

Our optimism affects the way we look at the rest of the world. We have built a nation that has become the global center of economic and military power. Rightly or wrongly, we imagine that if our influence could become even stronger throughout the world, the effect would be good. Oppressive[1] rulers would be replaced by responsible ones. Civil wars would stop. Women would be treated with dignity. Poverty would decline. On the other hand, if nations do not welcome American influence and American values, we are not optimistic about their futures.

---

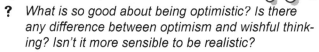

## Ask your American friends

### Opinions and experiences

? What is so good about being optimistic? Is there any difference between optimism and wishful thinking? Isn't it more sensible to be realistic?

? Do you think America gets into a lot of difficulty because it optimistically thinks it can fix problems in other countries even though those problems can never be fixed?

? How do you think other countries should try to be more like America? How would the world be better if they did?

### Other proverbs to discuss
(share some from your country too)

~ Every cloud has a silver lining.

~ No news is good news.

~ Lightning never strikes twice in the same place.

---

[1] **Oppressive** – using power unjustly

## UNSEEN POWERS; DESTINY

97. *(Commandment 10) God helps those who help themselves.* God looks favorably on people who take initiative. If you want something, work for it.

98. *In God we trust.* This motto is clearly displayed on every American coin and bill. It means many different things to different Americans.

99. *God bless America.* This prayer is also the title of a song often sung on patriotic occasions. Some politicians use it as the final line in a speech, especially when the issue is war.

100. *Time and tide wait for no man.* When something's time has come, it will happen and nothing can stop it. It is like an ocean tide coming in to the shore.

In many parts of the world, America is seen as a "Christian country." By comparison with most European countries, America is indeed very religious. Nevertheless we have no common proverbs that describe the greatness of God or instruct people to respect God. God is barely mentioned in our proverbs and when he is, he gets little credit for anything.

For example, we say, *God helps those who help themselves (97).* This can mean either that God will bless those who take initiative or that God is not a factor in how things turn out. The idea is that if one merely sits and prays but takes no actions, nothing good will happen.

It may appear that in America the real "god" (the ultimate center of attention and devotion) is the individual. Even many of the religious Americans try to get God to revolve around us, rather than adjusting our lives to revolve around God. We want God to meet our individual needs. We are not so interested in fitting into any divine master plan for the universe. The vast majority of us Americans say we believe in God but, crudely stated, we often act as if God is to be used, not worshipped.

What we appear to "worship," what we are powerfully drawn to and praise extravagantly, is not God but our "idols"—pop music stars, sports heroes, etc. A famous TV show is even called, "American Idol." We mentioned earlier that some people nearly worship money (p. 36).

We have a few proverbs about impersonal forces such as destiny, fate or history. We may say, Time and tide wait for no man (100), but these sayings are far outweighed by our proverbs on individual initiative. Americans want to believe that anything is possible through indi-vidual effort. We do not believe that fate, God, or any other unseen power has determined things and left us powerless to change them.

### Ask your American friends

#### Opinions and experiences

? *When you say,* God helps those who help themselves, *does that mean that you believe God really does help them or you do not believe God does anything, so people had better do things for themselves?*

**?** *I'm confused. Your money says, "In God We Trust," you sing, "God Bless America" at baseball games, but Americans do not seem to agree about who God is or what difference he makes. What difference does God make in America or in your life?*

**?** *My book says, "It may appear that the real 'god' in America is the individual person." What do you think that means? How true do you think it is?*

**?** *Who or what do you idolize? What attracts you so much to that person or thing?*

## Other proverbs to discuss

(share some from your country too)

~ *Marriages are made in heaven.*

~ *What will be will be.*

~ *The good die young.*

~ *Man proposes, God disposes.*

~ *You can't fool Mother Nature.*

**See also:** *The devil made me do it (72); History repeats itself (94).*

## Movies to watch and discuss

*Life of Pi* (2012 adventure drama, PG).
A young man searching for God loses his family in a shipwreck but survives in an epic journey on a lifeboat with a tiger. He maintains hope without finding "truth," leaving viewers to decide for themselves where is the dividing line between reality, illusion, and wish.

Other options: *The Passion; The Lion, the Witch, and the Wardrobe; Lord of the Rings; The Matrix*

**Conclusion**

# Time Will Tell

Like all cultures, American culture has some great strengths, some glaring weaknesses and some strange paradoxes. It may be too simplistic[1] to conclude that Americans are lonely super-achievers but there is some truth to that. We try to get everything without giving up anything, but it seems *you can't have your cake and eat it too (24)*.

Success, self-esteem and fun appear to be the most highly valued things in our culture. Love, money and "playing to win" are valued nearly as highly. Personal freedom and personal initiative make it possible for Americans to pursue these values.

While we are *looking out for number one (19)*, we give less attention to group loyalty, family relationships and sexual morality. All these tend to put limits on the individual pursuit of the primary values. As for God and fate, they get some attention but when they conflict with core cultural values, the core values usually take priority.

American culture is changing rapidly in areas such as gender roles, where there is no agreement about what is proper and desirable. It is

---

[1] **Simplistic** – explaining something only on the surface without really understanding it

hard to know what the next generation will do with the culture they inherit. It seems that they may be less achievement-oriented and more people-oriented than their parents. They certainly have more options, more money, more free time, and more teaching on self-esteem than any previous generation. How can it be that so many of them are still frustrated, bored, aimless, and taking drugs?

American culture assumes that if a society creates opportunities for its youth, everything else will turn out right. That assumption is not standing up well. America has not yet determined what else it needs or where else it should look. If America changes this basic assumption, the effects will spread through the whole culture and transform it, but in what direction? We do not know. We cannot find direction in sayings like *Just do it (39)* or *Go for it (3)*. They don't even tell us what "it" is.

America has vast wealth, technology, power and influence. It may be the best country in the world for shopping, having fun, or making your life a success. But is it the best country for "living"? Are we the freest people in the world and yet voluntary slaves to the clock and the credit card? Is consumerism the key to the good life or the start of the rat race? Is the whole American Dream *Too good to be true (9)? Time will tell (11)*.

# For Further Reading

This book is available in an expanded edition under the title, *American Cultural Baggage*  (Orbis Books, 2005), designed to help Americans become aware of their own culture before they go to work or live elsewhere. That version contains explanations of all the "other proverbs" listed at the ends of the sections in this book. It also gives longer explanations of the cultural values and many warnings for Americans who imagine they can live by their own culture no matter where they are.

Another helpful book is Sarah Lanier's work, *Foreign to Familiar: A Guide to Understanding Hot- and Cold-Climate Cultures,* available at www.mcdougalpublishing.com.

For those who want to dig deeper into the subject, see www.nicholasbrealey.com for many useful books such as *American Ways: A Cultural Guide to the United States (3rd ed.), Living in the USA (6th ed.),* and *American Cultural Patterns.*

# About the Author

Dr. Stan Nussbaum has been involved in cultural and religious research and training since 1977. Besides living in Lesotho (southern Africa) and England for seven years each, he has taught in many countries such as India, Korea, Malaysia, Nigeria, Uganda, Lithuania, Egypt, and Peru.

He has long held a special interest in proverbs as windows into a culture. He initiated and coordinated the African Proverbs Project, a four-year pan-African project funded by a research grant from The Pew Charitable Trusts.

Americans have a proverb, "Will it play in Peoria?" It means, "Will ordinary Americans like it?" Peoria is a small city in central Illinois, which is in the Midwest, and its people are considered typical of Americans. The author grew up seven miles from Peoria in the small town of Morton, where he returned in 2006 to take care of aging parents. He and his wife Lorri have two children and four grand-children, including the two to whom this book is dedicated.

# Alphabetical List of 100 Proverbs

*Please note*: The numbers in the following list refer to the number of the proverb, not the number of the page on which it is found.

---

A friend in need is a friend indeed.  # 58

A good captain goes down with his ship.  # 60

A man is only as old as he feels.  # 49

A man may work from sun to sun, but woman's work is never done.  # 52

A man's home is his castle.  # 51

A new broom sweeps clean.  # 92

All things come to him who waits.  # 47

An eye for an eye.  # 35

Are we having fun yet?  # 23

Birds of a feather flock together.  # 61

Boys will be boys.  # 55

Celebrate diversity.  # 53

Charity begins at home.  # 65

Do unto others as you would have them do to you.  # 70

Don't bite off more than you can chew.  # 12

Don't get mad, get even.  # 84

Don't put the cart before the horse.  # 7

**Enough is enough (Commandment 7).  # 68**

Fight fire with fire.  # 34

Get a life.  # 76

Give him an inch and he'll take a mile.  # 45

Go for it.  # 3

God bless America.  # 99

## God helps those who help themselves (Commandment 10). # 97

Half a loaf is better than no bread at all.  # 96
He who laughs last, laughs best.  # 83
History repeats itself.  # 94
Home is where the heart is.  # 67
Home, sweet home.  # 66

If it ain't broke, don't fix it.  # 46
If it feels good, do it.  # 22
If the shoe fits, wear it.  # 73
If you can't stand the heat, get out of the kitchen.  # 81
If you can't beat 'em, join 'em.  # 17
If you scratch my back, I'll scratch yours.  # 57
If you want something done right, do it yourself.  # 42
In God we trust.  # 98
Innocent until proven guilty.  # 71

## Just do it (Commandment 5).  # 39

Let a sleeping dog lie.  # 80
Let bygones be bygones.  # 85
Life, liberty and the pursuit of happiness.  # 36
**Live and let live (Commandment 2).  # 18**
Look before you leap.  # 8
Look on the bright side.  # 95
Looking out for number one.  # 19
Love conquers all.  # 27
Love finds a way.  # 28
Love makes the world go 'round.  # 29

Make it short and sweet.  # 90
Making every minute count.  # 87
Many hands make light work.  # 63
Misery loves company.  # 64

Money can't buy happiness.  # 31
Money talks.  # 30

Nice guys finish last.  # 33
No pain no gain.  # 44
Nobody is perfect.  # 54
Nothing succeeds like success.  # 2

Oh, for the vigor of youth again.  # 50
One bad apple can spoil the whole barrel.  # 56
One thing at a time.  # 5
Opportunity only knocks once.  # 88

Power corrupts.  # 79

Rats desert a sinking ship.  # 59
**Rules are made to be broken (Commandment 8).  # 77**

**Shop till you drop (Commandment 4).  # 25**
So far so good.  # 14
Stand on your own two feet.  # 41

The best defense is a good offense.  # 40
The customer is always right.  # 20
The devil made me do it.  # 72
The land of the free and the home of the brave.  # 37
The pot calling the kettle black.  # 75
The sooner the better.  # 89
The voice of the people is the voice of God.  # 78
There is no harm in trying.  # 43
There is no such thing as a free lunch.  # 10
There is safety in numbers.  # 62
There's many a slip between the cup and the lip.  # 4
Time and tide wait for no man.  # 100
**Time flies when you're having fun (Command-
     ment 3).  # 21**
**Time is money (Commandment 9).  # 86**

Time marches on.  # 91
Time will tell.  # 11
Tomorrow is another day.  # 93
Too good to be true.  # 9
Two wrongs don't make a right.  # 82
Variety is the spice of life.  # 26

We shall overcome.  # 38
We're number one.  # 32
What goes around comes around.  # 69
When in Rome, do as the Romans do.  # 6
When the going gets tough, the tough get going.  # 16
Where there's a will, there's a way.  # 13

Yes we can.  # 15
**You are only young once (Commandment 6).  # 48**
**You can't argue with success (Commandment 1).  # 1**
You can't have your cake and eat it too.  # 24
You made the bed, you lie in it.  # 74

# List of Cartoons

# List of Movies to Discuss

| Chapter Themes | Movies |
|---|---|
| 1. Overview | *Star Wars, p. 9* |
| 2. Success | *Forrest Gump, p. 20* |
| 3. Self-esteem | *Precious, p. 32* |
| 4. Playing to win | *The Searchers, p. 40* |
| 5. Freedom and initiative | *Finding Nemo, p. 50* |
| 6. Age, gender, human nature | *Cocoon, p. 58* |
| 7. Loyalty, groups, families | *E.T., the Extra-Terrestrial, p. 67* |
| 8. Fairness, blame, conflict | *Cool Hand Luke, p. 80* |
| 9. Time and change | *The Right Stuff, p. 87* |
| 10. Hope and God | *Life of Pi, p. 93* |

At the end of each chapter, one of the above movies is described and additional movies on each theme are listed. These movies were selected to include a wide spectrum of types of movies and a mix of current and classic movies. All are very famous movies, readily available for rental or purchase.

Not all the movies listed are suitable for children. If in doubt, check an on-line review of the movie or its description on *Wikipedia*, which always provides a summary in the "Plot" section of the article.

Made in the USA
Lexington, KY
06 January 2017